Prison Segmentation for Inner City Teacher Advisors

Phone, Video or Computer

Reverend Mike Wanner

Copyright
Rev. Mike Wanner, June 27, 2018

Selected Images Used by License

Table of Contents

Table of Contents 3
Introduction 4
1 - Why I am Writing This Book 5
2 - Where We Are 6
3 - Lemons to Lemonade 7
4 - Inner City Realities 8
5 - Language of Diversity Can Be Neutral 10
6 - The Value of Perspective 12
7 - Cultural Interpretation 13
8 - Inner-City Teachers Bridge 14
9 - Inner-City Culture Advisers 15
10 - Disconnected Agendas 16
11 - Structure of a Beneficial Collaboration 17
12 - Benefit for Teachers 18
13 - Benefit for Teacher's Students 19
14 - Benefit for Schools 20
15 - Benefit for Prisoners 22
16 - Benefit for Prisoner's Families, Prisons, and Taxpayers .. 23
17 - Reality Check 25
18 - Reality Counter Balancing Values 27
19 - Thank You 29
20 - Addendum 30
21 - Don't Worry Ever 31
22 - My Book Categories at Amazon 32
23 - Angels Please Prayers 33
24 - Private Channeling 34
25 - Reverend Mike Wanner 35

Introduction

It is Time for Challenging Changes

Inner city teachers can have their hands full, and part of that may be because of a reality void between television and the real world. There may be a tendency for safe and secure television viewers to expect that the real world is exciting and has no consequences.

Prisoners may have a different view and may wish to do something positive with the time they have on their sentences. Segmentation may allow prisoners to write about their adventures so they can share their experience and their recommendations.

It would be ideal if there was a program developed in segmentation that could allow that to happen through e-mail, phone, or video chats. Teachers could be invited to write for advice and then build a whole consultancy between prisoners and teachers.

How great it would be if a message or idea from prison changed the life of a young child.

1 - Why I am Writing This Book

Inner city children's lives can be very different from the lives of youth brought up in suburbia. There is a visible blending of communities that takes place over time, that mixing may be too slow for the highest potential of inner-city youth.

Youth is a formative time and lessons learned early may influence the life of the learner for many years to come. The highest and best may be what is wanted for every child of every parent, but the community influences may not align optimally with that goal.

It may be that educators with all the right credentials for teaching a child to succeed can also be less than optimal for a given child because of cultural miscommunications. The income of the citizens from the teachers' community and students' community may range from somewhat different to very different.

Resource differences may not be noticeable but may contribute to a kind of language meaning variation that needs a bit of translation so that participants both understand each other.

Teachers may not understand the inner-city subtleties. Prisoners may be a resource which can help bridge that gap.

Prisoners helping teachers and students could also help prisoners in the long run.

2 - Where We Are

**America is
Becoming Quite Desperate**
and it is
Time
Like Before the
Birth of Liberty
for clear thinking
and adventure
to mix enough with fiscal awareness,
guts, wisdom, determination, and
discernment
to create a path that can be walked
deliberately and precisely
from the chaos of the moment
to a Future with
Abundant Potential
For All.

3 - Lemons to Lemonade

Not

Exactly

But

The

Verbal

Image

Helps

To

See

Real

Options

For

Action

4 - Inner City Realities

Those who know both the music of the city vibe and the vibration of consequences may be just the right people to translate potentials between the two communities.

Citizens of the inner-city and suburbia both have highs and lows. They all interact and live in relative harmony more often than not.

Respect is such an essential component of co-habiting with people of different origins. I was blessed to be brought up in the City of Philadelphia where great diversity brings excellence and opportunity.

Philadelphia has fantastic institutions, Corporations, and services that are the envy of the world. We also have the contrast of those who are not doing as well as the whole community would like.

Building some bridges between schools and prisoner might just help the children in some schools that are related to the residents of some prisons. In the isolation of their controlled environments, there is likely a void on the understanding that could be filled by the project identified here,

Part of the curriculum could ask children of prisoners to write letters asking questions which invite answers that they and other children would like to know. The invitations could be structured as a community project with no one to expect a parental or personal response.

The invitation to the children could be in broad terms that ask a generic question. Perhaps something like the following.

Invitation to Children
Who have any questions About Prison, Prisoners, or why they cannot talk to a parent in prison.

This is a general invitation to ask questions so that answers can be assembled into a resource document for children who have family or friends who might be incarcerated. Collecting the answers to those questions can allow for batch answers that can be put in a book and shared with the participating schools to help present and future children of prisoners.

Separation from your parent for any reason can be severely stressful, so we want to help with some general answers to common questions.

The Book of Answers may soothe things a bit, allow you to get an answer in a way that is educational without the embarrassment of personal questions with no response.

Philadelphia could be an ideal location for an initial effort. Perhaps with some rethinking, we could change societies all over America by making some new historical answers to help children understand a little better.

5 - Language of Diversity Can Be Neutral

2.3 million prisoners in 6,000+ prisons and many stories make it clear to me that the influences of different cultures can become mixed with situational dynamics in an emotional way. Intense issues could be like a bright flame that does not mix well with gasoline and creates an explosion.

Human rage matched with reactive suppression and rigid thinking can also be explosive. Now we can ignore the realities and continue in the wrong direction, or we can start to investigate causation. I recommend the latter.

A significant factor in some prisons is gangs, and there is little done in beneficial ways to initiate remediation of the causes. It may be discovered that these groups fill a void in our society in ways that are not able to be understood because of cultural variations.

My whole life has been about understanding, and I recommend it heartily. I had a problem with God when I was young, and now I share that God can help with many issues.

Perspective can be invigorated with understanding to bless all who contribute to the conversation. Hopefully, this book will make some progress in all that is possible.

Many wars were waged where two factions had different views of what they perceived as Divine Inspiration. The God of us all is a God of Love and not war. We can revisit our understandings and change our reality.

How would prison be if we were able to single out candidates for societal healing who can bring awareness to the right issues at the right points in life for the right people to have better tomorrows? When we have enough right working to better the world, we will also have a society that can nurture people with less effort and more grace.

If somebody has an injury, they may be quick to seek medical attention. If ailments are ignored, some may heal, but many could get worse and cause further damage, illness, or death.

The size of our prison population is an indication that we have a sickness and or injury in our society. For some people, they can take charge of their circumstances enough to provide for themselves.

Everyone cannot do it for themselves, and there seems to be nowhere to go, and frustration can fester. Of course, we hear the arguments that the poor and disenfranchised bring their blight upon themselves and there may be some examples of that being partially correct.

The truth that I see is that too many people are outrageously self-centered. They do not even look at an effort to understand the problems of our society. As a result, problems get worse.

This book is about creating some win-win-win-win options for:
1. Urban Youth
2. Teachers
3. Prisoners
4. Taxpayers

6 - The Value of Perspective

Teachers may be confused when they do not get the positive reactions from the students that they might expect. There may be a gap as if the teacher had done something wrong.

Sometimes, what seems right is not. Sometimes what seems wrong is right.

Patience may serve a teacher well or not. Understanding can be difficult.

This book is about helping many people, including teachers, students, prisoners and the families of them all. There is an old bit of wisdom that contains the declaration that information is power.

That may be true at times but less than accurate at others. The appropriateness of the information application may be the key to the success of the application.

Teaching can be hard, and it can be gratifying. Education can also be comfortable and not satisfying.

Teachers can enjoy their work when they have the support they need or be challenged when they do not. We might be able to add some perspectives when we are able to add emotional translations to smooth situational relationships.

7 - Cultural Interpretation

Viewpoints are not criminal, but the emotional lockouts caused by a lack of understanding can get in the way of appropriately valuing what is said. Lack of clarity in communication can be problematic in learning and comprehension.

Sometimes it is essential to slow down enough so that everybody is on the same page at all levels of understanding. Little understanding lapses can impede education.

When a train is speeding down a track, and there is a piece of rail missing, there can be a train wreck. When a student cannot follow a train of thought, the consequences can be equally disastrous for that individual.

When an unfamiliar language is not understood, a listener may look for someone who speaks the unknown lingo so that comprehension of the words can be had. Cultural translations may not be so easily found.

Let us begin to seek ways to understand cultural gaps so that the intricacies of meaning are as easily translated as languages. I will cite an example in an addendum after the last chapter of a tool that can save lives for Non-English speakers in America today, maybe even some parents of children in the public schools.

Next, let's talk about culturally aware individuals helping teachers communicate more effectively now.

8 - Inner-City Teachers Bridge

For some teachers, their efforts at sharing and teaching may be mitigated somewhat by a lack of understanding. I sincerely believe that teachers try hard as do most students.

Viewpoints can influence word selection for teachers and students that complicate the teaching process. Awareness of any communication gaps may lead to facilitation of new ideas for clarity.

Please consider the possibility of prisoners to align with teachers of any classes where cultural enhancement awareness may benefit the students. The idea of all people created equal in the Declaration of Independence was and remains a unifying view of society.

Communication between all the equal people is an essential part of the understanding that will follow interactions. I want to encourage here some ideas that may assist prisoners and teachers and students and taxpayers.

School districts do not usually have enormous budgets for extra programs, but their student success levels could be enhanced by a progressive effort to learn from adult prisoners about the sensitivity that could have saved them from a life of crime.

All this could be a gift for prisoners to offer that would also help bring them an updated awareness of the outside world where someday they wish to go without feeling unwelcome.

9 - Inner-City Culture Advisers

What if we could create Volunteer Network teams of Teachers and prisoners who are willing to blog, chat, write about and otherwise share inner-city sensitivities.

Understanding is something that I always try to find in every situation. I have always been amazed at the different way that people look at things.

I have traveled to twenty-three countries and have seen so many variations of reasonable thinking. When I ask questions that I may think are "dumb," the revelation is always much different than I could ever expect.

Of course, I am one who asks questions, and there is a reason that I do. Asking questions is the only way that I change paradigms or perspectives, or understand the foundational concepts of anything or everything.

If I accepted that there would be no value in asking and then did not do it, my foundation for writing and understanding would be less stable.

I sincerely hope that there is much more here than the asking and answering. I hope the process brings a new level of understanding and new possibilities for prisoners, prison staff, teachers, students and the families of them all and all the communities they live within.

10 - Disconnected Agendas

Imagine please if we could prepare interactivity between the community and the schools and prisons and the prisoners and the prison staff and their families which could have the following potential future benefits:

1. Teachers who understand the community they teach in better.

2. Prisoners who have supported understanding between the teachers and the community members.

3. Teachers who are less stressed because they understand more than they previously did.

4. Prisoners who have the opportunity to provide a purpose and service to the outside community.

5. Inner-city students who went wrong can now have the non-academic understanding to share their perspectives with the academics.

6. Prison staff who have prisoners who are focused on doing good.

7. An improvement process rooted in full communication.

11 - Structure of a Beneficial Collaboration

Prisons could offer Inner-city schools the opportunity to receive feedback on a variety of underserved groups or interest areas. Projects could start with a request for sensitive response relevant to a target area where teachers feel the need for support.

Host facilities could establish their own group list but some areas to consider might be

1. Minority interests in Religions.

2. Minority interests in Cultural Diversity.

3. Minority interests in Ethnic Diversity

4. Minority interests in Languages

5. Minority interests in Survival Skillsets for Inner-City Students,

6. Minority interests for Children of Prisoners.

7. Minority interests for Medical Minorities

8. Minority interests for Disabled Students

9. Minority interests for Socially Challenged students

12 - Benefit for Teachers

This may or may not work for teachers depending on many factors that could vary from the traditional to the entirely unusual. Schools have a lot of struggles that can run the gamut and there seem to be not-enough subtle supports for everybody.

The administration could block the idea at the prison or at the school, and there may be no progress towards the concept, so please do not get ahead of yourself. When change is needed, patience is a beautiful virtue.

The emotionality at each class level can change especially when the income level of the families is significantly different. If this program has some appeal for teachers, then there is value for everybody as a teacher can see the holistic class impact perspective.

Teachers are expected by many to have the inside track on everything, and it may be likely that they are harder on themselves than they really need be. Having to support themselves without perspective enhancement when questions come up can bring a real sense of struggle.

Feeling supported could really enhance the peace and perspective of teachers and eventually their productivity and the success of their students.

A little progress could make a big statement about the values the system encourages.

13 - Benefit for Teacher's Students

Teachers are not entertainers as their role is to impart knowledge, but being peaceful in their relationships with students is a plus. To the degree that each interaction is smooth and confident, the satisfaction of the participants may be more beneficial and educational.

Each teacher has the opportunity to plant seeds in each student's garden of knowledge so that they are well equipped to adjust to the challenges of life. To the degree that teachers can adapt to many things quickly and appropriately can balance their reactions with a level of optimal fluidity.

The hope would be that teachers could have a resource to advise them on how to approach students with sensitivity and understanding.

Benefit for Teacher's Schools

Schools are agencies of the governing authorities and their performance at satisfying the needs of the communities are essential to the communal valuation of success.

Benefit for Teacher's Families

The families of teachers may have a not so subtle desire for their beloved to be respected in their roles, radiate their success and fulfill the potential opportunities of their students.

14 - Benefit for Schools

Freeing Teachers Reduces Stress For All

Teachers have essential assignments, and parts of their jobs may not be as satisfying as they could be. Standard operating procedure at our schools may have teachers spending much of their valuable time as a hall or room monitors.

Tedious functions may complicate the teacher's lives and waste expensive time that could be more productive elsewhere.
The roles of teachers have evolved over time, and there is a lot that they do.

Progress in many things is determined by things along the way that may not be seen outside of the internal decision sessions.

If we could remove tedious functions from teachers by assigning some basic tasks to prisoner advisers, we could free up their time and their talents for work that can serve the student community better. To do that, we need to open our minds to changes that could enhance the dignity and respect for both groups.

Redefinition of possibilities can serve us well in that regard. The way that things have always been done is not the end of the discussion.

Let us focus on goals that have the potential to achieve higher purpose and satisfaction. Optimal Employment and opportunity are worthy goals.

Consider please if the reader and the community can conceive secure plans for realigning functions to:

1. Provide Optimal information for students and teachers and others.

2. Deliver safe activities for prisoner involvement.

3. Optimize the understanding of teachers about those students of various cultures who could be better served if teachers have relevant information.

4. Reducing prisoner boredom.

5. Give Opportunities for personal growth for prisoners, teacher, and students.

6. Proposals that can free teachers from tedious pursuits can maintain a status quo with an optimized plan.

15 - Benefit for Prisoners

Prisoners having an active connection with the world outside the walls could update the prisoner's view of current day realities in the outside world and predispose them to their own success upon reentry.

Owning a favorable view of a future that can enable opportunities that have never even been perceived can be an excellent course correction for the journey of the prisoner.

Working with teachers could build a pipeline of awareness that could begin to promote understanding in new ways for many people. Prisoners who have children and have been struggling with the loss of connectivity may find some solace in helping the teachers of other prisoners to understand the needs of the children of all prisoners,

Participating in a program could help to form a template where some prisoners children could be supported by the project that furthers the design and implementation of the project that may eventually help children who are in the communities where their children came from.

Additionally, the idea of purpose as part of motivation can help assure that they can do some good and benefit society in a new way.

16 - Benefit for Prisoner's Families, Prisons, and Taxpayers

Benefit for Prisoner's Families

Prisoners occupied by programs that benefit the community allow prisoners to turn away from other efforts that fill their' incarcerated time with little or no long-term benefit. Meaningful service can go a long way to soothe the old emotional hurts that may have been the cause of the prisoner choosing the wrong path that brought them to prison.

Everything that can be done in prison to bring positivity to the world of the prisoner can help prepare them for the readjustments that they will need upon reentry.

Benefit for Prisons

The positive focus for the prisoners is therapeutic in its own right and what comes around can go around further and continue to bless others with positive awareness. As each individual raises their level of connectivity, it can set the stage well for their reentry and their ability to get out and stay out.

Peaceful patient prisoners can be a lot easier to work with than agitated residents who are looking to get back at somebody for something. Peace in the place can be a platform for the efforts of all who are trying to make things better.

Benefit for Taxpayers

Prisons are expensive, and taxpayers have a substantial burden every year in funding each active cell. When we can cut costs, the charges to the taxpayers can be less, and there can be more money for other programs that can benefit the rest of the citizens in the governmental district.

The government in every jurisdiction has a limited ability to tax, so frugality is essential. Also significant is the value that is effective for the mitigation of future expenses and quality of life for all residents that need to be in prison.

The government also needs to learn what will diminish a need for prisons with active educational systems and judiciary proceedings designed to discern the balance as well and effectively as possible.

17 - Reality Check

The sharing of this concept has many intentions which include:

1. Raising the level of engagement for prisoners as to doing something that can increase the prisoner's connectedness with the community.

2. Provide support for the children of prisoners who may not be well served because of their parental standing.

3. Providing hope for future prisoners' possibilities and readiness to deal effectively in a changing environment.

4. Changing the focus of prisoners from I to we when possible.

5. Raising the awareness within the community of the children faces standing in the shadows and struggling to find their place.

6. Bring bittersweet emotional reality to the prisoners so they can process the challenge that they and their children may face at all levels.

7. Shift the idea of reentry into something that needs to be prepared for in advance of reentry.

8. Make reentry a family deal that can help for many families.

9. Provide a difficulty evaluation to the prisoners about the future.

10. Wet the awareness of specific skills that will be needed in order to stand a chance at survival.

11. Bring awareness that they will need a B plan and C Plan. The efforts worked may have provided impetus and engagement and increased sensitivity.

12. The following realities may impede any thoughts that the educational loop is appropriate for them unless they create options that the schools can embrace:

    a. School Districts are challenged with the safety of children so any direct contact with children will likely not be authorized.

    b. Teaching children is a highly credentialed field, and most prisoners are likely not adequately credentialed, and those who may be might not be considered because of their incarceration.

13. Programs for parents and teachers are unlikely to be seen as potential programs for prisoners and ex-prisoners to target. Creativity could be just the ticket to open unexpected potentials to educate the adults in ways they can cooperate to serve the children better.

18 - Reality Counter Balancing Values

The needs of schools are enormous and the right plans initiated the right ways to the right schools at the right times could have success potential. Please note that nothing here is sugar-coated because your prospects could be very glum the way things are outside now and the chances of you lucking out are remote.

Just like your efforts to consult with teachers are separate from teachers physically, you may design your own separation and security into a system that you develop for children.

The primary issue for you re-entering the community will likely be housing, work, feeding your family and staying out of trouble.

Try to design a system for yourself in prison that is transferable when you go outside. In order to do that, there must be value for you as a provider that is not available elsewhere.

Value of your services in prison at the prison-rates will not allow you to survive outside of jail so you will need to get creative in order to keep your customer after you exit. Your program will need to be soup to nuts so consider developing tiers that will have you as a free citizen overseeing tomorrows prisoners while reaping a value that is between prison rates and civilian never-incarcerated person rates.

Even if you never develop an after-prison plan, your work on the inside could prepare you adequately for success. Helping the children and schools could improve your life forever.

And

Services to consider for development may be to provide identical inside prison programs and after-prison programs, so that cost containment and value serve all parties and offer new opportunities for a new standard of service that fills apparent needs that are not addressed now. Services to consider may be:

1. School Hall remote monitoring for security and good order.

2. Remote Detention supervision with quantitative evaluation of discipline compliance.

3. Remote Study hall supervision.

4. Remote Test-taking supervision and certification.

5. Remote School property access and egress.

6. Remote Schoolyard confrontations recording.

7. Remote Handicap bathroom access.

8. Multi-step pricing to provide many value.

It will be a great day for America when we are able to have prisoner advised Teachers able to wet the educational appetites of their students with information that will help all of them to better interact with the community.

19 - Thank You

For
Considering
These
Ideas

20 - Addendum

A Language Tool That Can Help In Medical Crises

There are 145 languages spoken just in Philadelphia (205 More throughout America.) As one who has done ambulance work and ministry in Philadelphia, I want to share a FREE medical tool that can help those who do not speak English who may have a medical emergency one day.

The tool can be found at the website http://angelraphaelspeaks.com/non-eng-med-hist/

The idea is simple. Friends or family members of the Non-English speaker can fill out the form for the one who might need it someday.

The form identifies the person, the **Language They Speak**, and their full medical history, so there is a starting point for the doctors when they are taken to a hospital. That information and the vital signs taken upon arrival can be enough to allow the doctors to save the life of a prepared person. No Info = Risk.

That simple form can help many Philadelphia residents, and you can use it also in your neighborhood to support any of the Non-English speakers who speak any of the 350 Languages spoken in America.

This is also important to English speakers because delays in the care of those ahead of you in a hospital queue can slow the arrival of your care.

21 - Don't Worry Ever

Ever

It Does Not Help Prayer Still Does!

Resource: http://Create-A-Prayer.com

22 - My Book Categories at Amazon

Distant Healing (or Mail List) e-mail mikewann@voicenet.com

Veterans Healing Six Pack plus 2
http://angelraphaelspeaks.com/healing-books/veterans/

PTSD Power Pack
http://angelraphaelspeaks.com/healing-books/ptsd/

Angel Raphael Speaks Series & Other Angel Books
http://angelraphaelspeaks.com/

Reiki
http://angelraphaelspeaks.com/healing-books/reiki/

Children
http://angelraphaelspeaks.com/healing-books/children/

Emergency Medical Kindness
http://angelraphaelspeaks.com/healing-books/emergency-medical-kindness/

Cancer
http://angelraphaelspeaks.com/healing-books/cancer/

Addictions
http://angelraphaelspeaks.com/healing-books/addictions/

Miscellaneous Healing
http://angelraphaelspeaks.com/healing-books/misc-healing/

Prison Books - 50+ Prison Books
http://angelraphaelspeaks.com/prison-books/

23 - Angels Please Prayers

Addict's
Angels of Healing Selected
Help Me to Stay Directed
Come To Me From The Sky
I Am Ready to Succeed Not Try
If I Don't Invite You In
I Might Not Win
I Have Been Lost For Too Long
Help Me To Stay Strong

Alcoholic's
Angels of Healing On High
Help Me to Stay Dry
Come To Me From The Sky
I Am Ready to Succeed Not Try
If I Don't Invite You In
I Might Not Win
I Have Been Lost For Too Long
Help Me To Stay Strong

From

http://AngelRaphaelSpeaks.com/AAAAAAA/
The Link Above Has the Core Messages from the book on drop-down pages.

24 - Private Channeling

Angel Raphael Speaks a series of free messages that are channeled through Reverend Mike Wanner for the Highest good and Highest Healing of all concerned.

Many questions arise about Reverend Mike doing private channeling, and he does help with that so E-mail him.

Reverend Mike is available worldwide as a psychic channel, emotional release facilitator, spiritual energy practitioner & teacher, and public speaker. He looks forward to meeting you soon! Email - mikewann@voicenet.com 215-342-1270

Private Spiritual Readings/channelings or Spiritual Healing Sessions: Telephone or in person.

Rev. Mike is available for individual, intuitive one-on-one sessions with you, his Guide Family, and your Guides. He helps by offering clarity on emotional situations about your life, your purpose, your spirituality, and your release of stuffed emotions and cellular memory.

Connect to the love of your Guides today!

For more information, Please visit

http://angelraphaelspeaks.com/channel/

25 - Reverend Mike Wanner

Rev. Mike Wanner started his spiritual and ministerial studies with Reiki in 1993 and had studied seven styles of Reiki in the U.S., Japan, Canada, Denmark, and Australia. He is certified to teach. He became certified to teach Integrated Energy Therapy in 1999 and co-taught the first IET class of the new Millennium. Mike began dowsing in 2001.

Ordained as an Interfaith Minister of the Circle of Miracles Ministry and a Metaphysical Minister of the International Metaphysical Ministry, Rev. Mike practices and teaches spiritual energy therapies in the Philadelphia Area.

Rev. Mike holds ministerial degrees from the University of Metaphysics and the University of Sedona. He is a Pastoral Care Associate at Jefferson - Frankford Hospital. He taught at the National Academy of Massage Therapy and Health Sciences.

Rev. Mike was a faculty member of the Medical Mission Sister's Center for Human Integration's School of Integrated Body/Mind Therapies in Fox Chase, Philadelphia, PA for twelve years.

For a complete Biography, Please visit
http://ReverendMikeWanner.com/Bio

www.ingramcontent.com/pod-product-compliance
Lightning Source LLC
Chambersburg PA
CBHW030121230526
45469CB00005B/1741